D0747113

DAY HIKES ON
KAUAI

by Robert Stone

Photographs by Robert Stone
Published by:
Day Hike Books, Inc.
114 South Hauser Box 865
Red Lodge, MT 59068
Layout & Design: Paula Doherty
Copyright 1997
Library of Congress Catalog Card Number: 96-96512

Distributed by:
ICS Books, Inc.
1370 E. 86th Place
Merrillville, IN 46410
1-800-541-7323
Fax 1-800-336-8334

TABLE OF CONTENTS

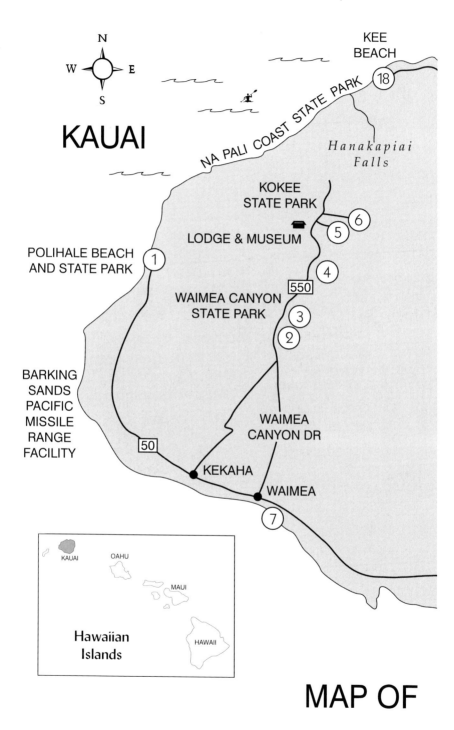

KAUAI

KEE
BEACH

NA PALI COAST STATE PARK

Hanakapiai
Falls

KOKEE
STATE PARK

LODGE & MUSEUM

POLIHALE BEACH
AND STATE PARK

WAIMEA CANYON
STATE PARK

550

BARKING
SANDS
PACIFIC
MISSILE
RANGE
FACILITY

50

WAIMEA
CANYON DR

KEKAHA

WAIMEA

Hawaiian
Islands

KAUAI   OAHU

MAUI

HAWAII

MAP OF

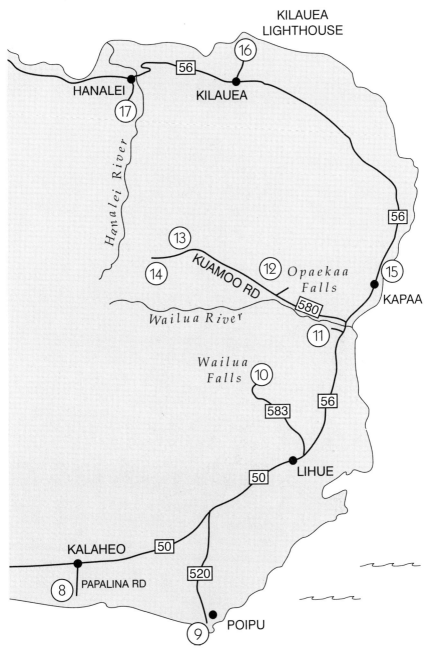

THE HIKES

About the Hikes

The Hawaiian Islands are among the most beautiful and dramatic tropical landscapes on earth. Located in the Pacific Ocean, Hawaii is 500 miles from any other island and 2,500 miles from the nearest continent. With its stunning, varied scenery and wide range of activities, Hawaii has something for everyone. The landscape is covered with verdant green mountains, active and dormant volcanoes, remote canyons, rain forests, lush flora and fauna, countless waterfalls, colored sand beaches, and coral reefs. Warm, turquoise ocean water surrounds the islands. The temperature hovers around 80 degrees with sunshine and gentle winds. Trade winds buffet the northeast side of each island, creating dense rain forests and exotic tropical plants. The southwest region of each island has barren, desert-like terrain, including cactus plants. There is a rich ethnic diversity of people, great food, music, and dance. The islands offer easy access to swimming, snorkeling, scuba diving, wind surfing, sailing, kayaking, canoeing, rafting, fishing, sunbathing, bicycling, people watching, and hiking.

The Day Hikes guide to Kauai focuses on scenic day hikes of various lengths. My goal is to share these hikes with you and others, enabling visitors as well as locals to see the diversity of this Hawaiian Island and enjoy the backcountry with ease. These hikes offer a variety of lush valleys, spectacular waterfalls, botanical gardens, arboretums, swimming holes, tropical streams, rain forests, and ridge trails with views.

The verdant "Garden Isle" of Kauai is an emerald green gem of lush foliage, cascading waterfalls, dramatic valleys, and canyons. The 553-square mile island of Kauai is Hawaii's oldest and northernmost island. Mount Waialeale, the wettest place on earth, averages 451 inches of rain annually. It is the source of many of Kauai's waterfalls. Seven rivers originate from Mount Waialeale and flow to the ocean. Nearly half of the 335,000-acre island is mountainous forest, accessible only by hiking trails. It is no wonder this exotic island has caught the eye of Hollywood. Films such as *South Pacific, Blue Hawaii, The Thornbirds, Raiders of the Lost Ark, Jurassic Park,* and *King Kong* were filmed here.

Na Pali State Park on the northwest coast of Kauai takes in more than 6,000 acres. The awesome Na Pali Coastline has imposing perpendicular cliffs which plunge 4,000 feet to the cobalt blue Pacific Ocean and is accessible only by trail. A hiking trail hugs the coastline while winding along these cliffs into Kalalau Valley. The trail begins at the end of the road by Kee Beach.

Along the tropical north shore are quaint one-lane bridges, rainbows, and charming serene villages with weathered houses, flowering gardens, and overgrown hedges of hibiscus and plumeria. White sand beaches line a variety of beautiful bays, including the horseshoe-shaped Hanalei Bay. On the northern-most point of Kauai is the 52-foot Kilauea Lighthouse, built in 1913 and now within the Kilauea National Wildlife Refuge. Located on a peninsula overlooking the ocean this towering cliff are colonies of Red Footed Boobies and other birds inhabiting the neighboring cliffs.

The colossal Waimea Canyon, known as the Grand Canyon of the Pacific, is 10 miles in length with glowing jewel-colored cathedral walls which descend 3,000 feet. The cool, wet, high country of Kokee State Park, adjacent to Waimea Canyon, is a lush 4,300-acre wilderness preserve with more than 40 miles of hiking trails and fresh water streams. The trails wind through the forest and along the canyon rim.

Polihale State Park is a two-mile strip of sandy beach on the dry west coast of Kauai. The park's sheer, majestic grey cliffs and jagged peaks rise above the wide stretch of white sand and the deep blue ocean beyond. The park has picnic facilities and is an ideal spot for viewing sunsets.

The Wailua River on the east coast is Hawaii's only navigable river. Riverboat rides go up the river through exotic plant forests to the Fern Grotto, a 40-foot cavern draped and covered in ferns. Inland from the Wailua River is Opaekaa Falls and a variety of hiking trails at Nounou Mountain (known as "The Sleeping Giant"), Kuilau Ridge, and the Keahua Arboretum.

Along the dry, sunny south coast of Kauai are the crescent-shaped white sand beaches of Poipu, protected by offshore reefs. It is a popular tourist destination with tide pools, blowholes, and excellent snorkeling. Lihue, the largest city and county seat, is home to Kauai's airport. Near Lihue is Wailua Falls, a twin cascade plunging 80 feet into a pool.

All of the hikes listed in this guide require easy to moderate effort and are timed at a leisurely rate. If you wish to hike faster or go further, set your own pace accordingly. As I hike, I enjoy looking at clouds, rocks, insects, wildflowers, streams, vistas, and any other subtle pleasures of nature. While this adds to the time, it also adds to the experience.

The major access roads to all these hikes are Highway 50, heading south and west along the perimeter out of Lihue, and Highway 56, heading north and west along the perimeter, also out of Lihue. The highway markers roughly correspond with mileage distances in each direction beginning in Lihue at mile marker "0." The driving distances throughout the book will be measured from Lihue. The elevations of the hikes range between sea level and 3,000 feet.

As for attire and equipment, tennis shoes, as opposed to hiking boots, are fine for any of these hikes. A rain poncho, sunscreen, and mosquito repellent are recommended. Drinking water is a must. The trails can be (and usually are) slippery due to rain and mud, so use caution. Pack a lunch for a picnic at scenic outlooks, streams, pools, or wherever you find the best spot.

Enjoy your hike!

Hike 1
Polihale Beach and State Park

Hiking Distance: 0.5 to 4 miles round trip
Hiking Time: 1 to 3 hours
Elevation Gain: Level hiking

Summary of hike: Polihale Beach and State Park is a long, beautiful, open sand beach at the south edge of the Na Pali cliffs. You may walk along this leeward coast in solitude for miles.

Driving directions: From Lihue, drive 39 miles west on Highway 50 to the end of the road, seven miles past the town of Kekaha. Shortly after the Pacific Missile Range Facility, the road forks. Take the fork to the right (east) for 0.5 miles to the first left turn. Turn left, as the sign directs, onto a cane field road. Continue 1.8 miles to the end of the road and turn left. Drive toward the ocean 3.1 miles to the Polihale "day use" parking area. Turn left and park.

Hiking directions: From the parking area, walk toward the ocean. To the right are the Na Pali cliffs, which are fascinating to explore. To the left is a long expanse of beach that stretches for miles. Follow this coastline towards Barking Sands beach and sand dunes. Along the way, cool off with a swim in the ocean. The Pacific Missile Range Facility is two miles down the beach, which you cannot miss, and is a good place to turn around.

Waimea Canyon and Kokee State Park

Waimea Canyon and Kokee State Park, referred to as the "Grand Canyon of the Pacific," have an extensive network of hiking trails. The canyon has more than 45 miles of trails and measures ten miles long by one mile wide with a depth of 3,000 feet (photo on back cover).

Instead of overwhelming the visitor with 20-plus hikes, I have included five hikes which offer an excellent cross-section of all that this multicolored canyon has to offer. The views into this ancient and richly colored canyon highlight the layers of black, red, purple, and pink rock framed by the changing cloud formations (back cover photo). These selected hikes have a variety of scenic overlooks from the rim into the canyon, deep jungle trails with lush vegetation, streams, waterfalls, and swimming pools. Wild pigs and goats may be spotted on any of these hikes.

The driving directions to each of these trails are given from both the coast and from Kokee Lodge and Kokee Natural History Museum. The forested plateau of Kokee State Park has a lodge with cabin rentals and a restaurant. Next to the lodge is a superb museum offering everything you would want to know about the area, plus a gift shop with books and maps.

Due to the frequency of rain in this area, it is not advisable to drive on unpaved roads with two-wheel drive vehicles. Doing so could lead to a "day hike" back to civilization.

Hike 2
Waimea Canyon and Kokee State Park
Iliau Nature Loop

Hiking Distance: 0.3 mile loop
Hiking Time: 15 minutes
Elevation Gain: Level hiking

Summary of hike: This hike is a short, self-guided loop and identifies a variety of native plants in the area. The trail has a picnic shelter and lookout areas into Waimea Canyon. Directly across the canyon is Waialae Falls.

Driving directions: From Lihue, drive 26.5 miles west on Highway 50 to Highway 550 in the town of Kekaha. Turn right towards Waimea Canyon. Drive north 9.8 miles. The trailhead will be on the right.

If you are starting from Kokee Lodge and Museum, drive 6.9 miles down the canyon (south) to the trailhead on the left. Parking pullouts are on the west side of the road, directly across from the trailhead.

Hiking directions: From the trailhead, follow the trail to the right for 100 yards to a junction. Take the left trail, which winds counterclockwise along the Iliau Nature Loop. The right trail descends into the canyon along the Kukui Trail (Hike 3). As the trail loops along the canyon rim, there are various views into and across the canyon before it leads back to the parking area.

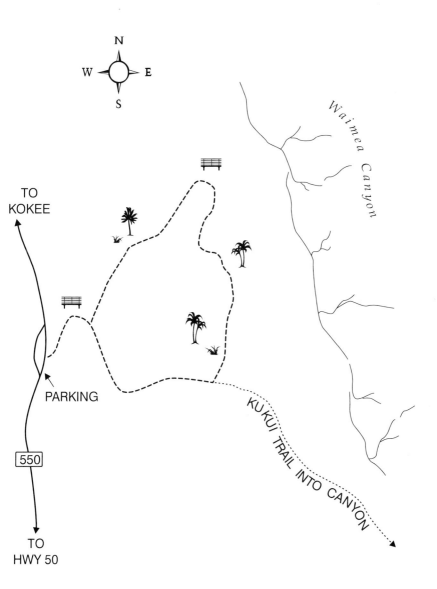

ILIAU NATURE LOOP

Hike 3
Waimea Canyon and Kokee State Park
Kukui Trail to Overlooks

Hiking Distance: 2 miles round trip
Hiking Time: 1.5 hours
Elevation Gain: 750 feet

Summary of hike: This hike descends part way into Waimea Canyon with spectacular views and a perspective from inside the canyon (photo on page 19). Across the canyon are several waterfalls that stay in view along the one-mile descent. The predominant waterfall is Waialae Falls. Wild goats are frequently visible along the canyon ridges.

Driving directions: From Lihue, drive 26.5 miles west on Highway 50 to Highway 550 in the town of Kekaha. Turn right towards Waimea Canyon. Drive 9.8 miles. The trailhead is on the right.

If you are starting from Kokee Lodge and Museum, drive 6.9 miles down the canyon (south) to the trailhead on the left. Parking pullouts are on the left side of the road, across from the trailhead.

Hiking directions: From the trailhead, the trail leads to the right along the beginning portion of the Iliau Nature Loop (Hike 2). After 100 yards, is a junction with a trail sign directing you to the right. (Heading left winds through the Nature Loop.) Continue on the Kukui Trail to the right. Follow the switchbacks less than 1/4 mile to the first viewing area, graced with a bench. There are metal 1/4 mile markers along the trail. Every step takes you deeper into the canyon and offers a changing view and perspective. Continue down to the second viewing area with a bench, at about the one-mile marker. Although the Kukui Trail descends more than 2,300 feet to the Waimea River on the canyon floor, this second viewing area is used as our turnaround point. To return, climb back up and out of the canyon.

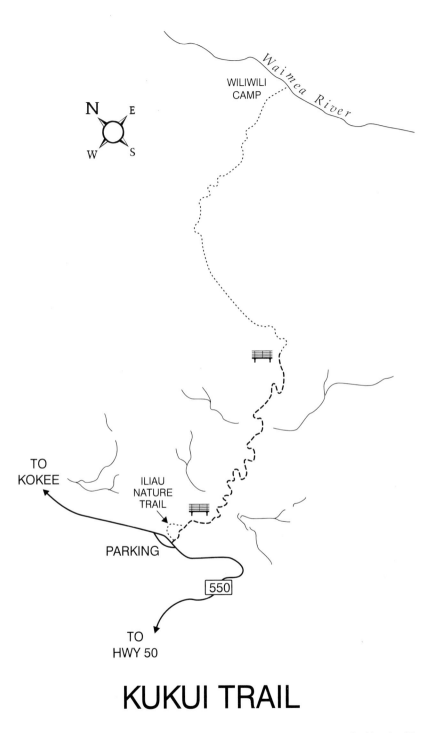

KUKUI TRAIL

Hike 4
Waimea Canyon and Kokee State Park
Upper and Lower Waipoo Falls
Canyon Trail

Hiking Distance: 3.2 miles round trip
Hiking Time: 2 hours
Elevation Gain: 600 feet

Summary of hike: Upper and Lower Waipoo Falls offer a cool retreat for hikers. Upper Waipoo Falls is fronted by a swimming pool. Lower Waipoo Falls has showering cascades and several small soaking pools. The hike to the falls on Canyon Trail is equally enjoyable, offering magnificent views as it descends into Waimea Canyon. A short side trip along Cliff Trail also offers tremendous views of the canyon.

Driving directions: From Lihue, drive 26.5 miles west on Highway 50 to Highway 550 in the town of Kekaha. Turn right towards Waimea Canyon. Drive north 15.5 miles to the trailhead (on the right) at Halemanu Road.

If you are starting from Kokee Lodge and Museum, drive 1.4 miles down the canyon (south) to the trailhead (on the left) at Halemanu Road. Parking is available on both sides of the road.

Hiking directions: From the parking area, hike down Halemanu Road 0.8 miles to the trailhead. A marked trail junction will direct you to Canyon and Black Pipe Trails. About 100 yards down the trail is a second junction. To the left is Canyon Trail, which is our main route. (Cliff Trail is the trail to the right and continues a short distance to a beautiful overlook of Waimea Canyon.) Continue down Canyon Trail as it descends 0.3 miles to the Black Pipe Trail junction. Stay on Canyon Trail as it bears right and levels out onto a large bare knoll overlooking the canyon. The trail picks up again at the lower edge of the knoll and veers to the left. Lower Waipoo Falls is a short distance ahead at a T-junction. The Upper Falls are to the left. The main trail, to the right, leads to the Lower Falls. Return to your car along the same trail.

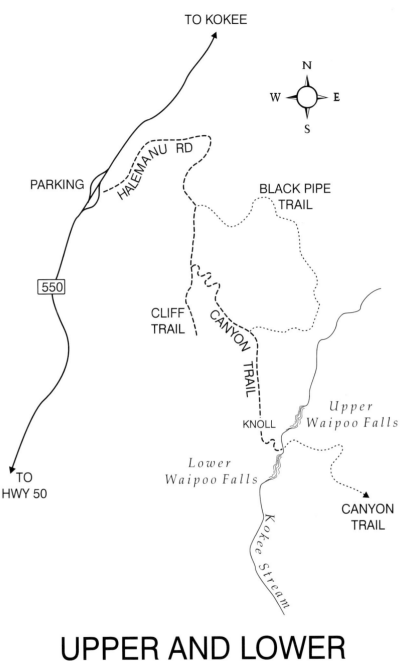

TO KOKEE

N
W E
S

PARKING

HALEMANU RD

550

BLACK PIPE
TRAIL

CLIFF
TRAIL

CANYON TRAIL

TO
HWY 50

KNOLL

*Upper
Waipoo Falls*

*Lower
Waipoo Falls*

CANYON
TRAIL

Kokee Stream

UPPER AND LOWER
WAIPOO FALLS

Opaekaa Falls - Hike 14

Taro fields en route to Hanalei River - Hike 17

View of Kalalau Valley from Kokee State Park

Kukui Trail and view into Waimea Canyon – Hike 3

Hike 5
Waimea Canyon and Kokee State Park
Halemanu-Kokee Trail

Hiking Distance: 2.4 miles round trip
Hiking Time: 1.5 hours
Elevation Gain: 300 feet

Summary of hike: This hike is on a pleasant, well-groomed, easy trail abundant with plant life and blackberries when in season. It connects Camp 10 Road and Halemanu Road through a beautiful 1.2 mile koa forest.

Driving directions: From Lihue, drive 26.5 miles west on Highway 50 to Highway 550 in the town of Kekaha. Turn right towards Waimea Canyon. Drive north 16.8 miles, just past Kokee Lodge and Museum.

If you are starting from Kokee Lodge and Museum, drive 0.1 mile on Highway 550 to Camp 10 Road. This is the first right turn past the lodge, and it is marked with the sign "Kumuwela Road," which is actually Camp 10 Road. Turn right on this road and drive 0.5 miles to the "Camp Sloggett" sign posted on the right. Turn right and continue 0.1 mile. Park by the old ranger station. The trailhead is on the right, just before the building, and is identified with a sign.

Hiking directions: From the trailhead, hike southwest. The well-defined trail is fairly level for the first mile. Near the end, the trail goes downhill and meets the Halemanu Road. Return along the same path.

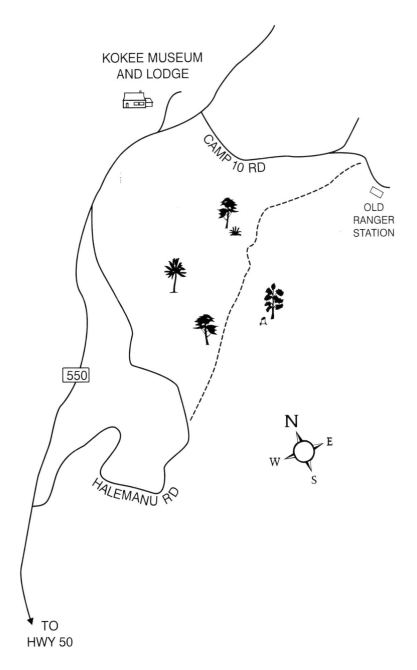

KOKEE MUSEUM
AND LODGE

CAMP 10 RD

OLD
RANGER
STATION

550

HALEMANU RD

N
W E
S

TO
HWY 50

HALEMANU-KOKEE TRAIL

Ocean view at Poipu Beach - Hike 9

Lily pond and bridge at Botanical Gardens - Hike 11

Mokuaeae Island at Kilauea Point Wildlife Refuge - Hike 16

Japanese garden at Kukuiolono Park - Hike 8

Hike 6
Waimea Canyon and Kokee State Park
Kumuwela Trail

Hiking Distance: 1.6 miles round trip
Hiking Time: 1 hour
Elevation Gain: 350 feet

Summary of hike: This is a true jungle hike, yet the trail is easy to follow. You will feel dwarfed by the dense, towering vegetation. The Kumuwela Trail connects the Camp 10 Road and the Kumuwela Road.

Driving directions: From Lihue, drive 26.5 miles west on Highway 50 to Highway 550 in the town of Kekaha. Turn right towards Waimea Canyon. Drive north 16.8 miles, just past Kokee Lodge and Museum.

If you are starting from Kokee Lodge and Museum, drive 0.1 mile on Highway 550 to Camp 10 Road. This is the first right turn past the lodge, and it is marked with the sign "Kumuwela Road," which is actually Camp 10 Road. Turn right on this road and drive 0.5 miles to the "Camp Sloggett" sign posted on the right. Turn right and drive another 0.6 miles to the end of the road. The trailhead is on the left.

Hiking directions: From the trailhead, which is marked with a sign, hike south. Once on the trail, you will descend into the vine-covered forest past ferns and fragrant Kahili ginger. At times you will hear Kokee Stream to the right. Continue 0.8 miles to the end of the trail where it intersects with Kumuwela Road. Return along the same path.

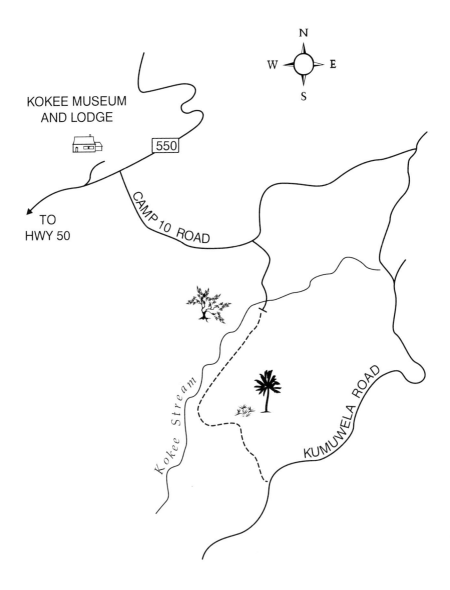

KOKEE MUSEUM
AND LODGE

550

TO
HWY 50

CAMP 10 ROAD

N
W E
S

Kokee Stream

KUMUWELA ROAD

KUMUWELA TRAIL

Hike 7
Russian Fort State Park

Hiking Distance: 1 mile loop
Hiking Time: 30 minutes
Elevation Gain: Level hiking

Summary of hike: The Russian Fort State Park is located at the mouth of the Waimea River overlooking the ocean. The fort's red rock walls were constructed in the early 1800s and were originally twelve feet high. Built without mortar, the fort is crumbling and fragile. The shell of the fort is all that remains, so bring your imagination.

Driving directions: From Lihue, drive 22.5 miles west on Highway 50. A sign is posted on the highway at the fort's entrance. Turn left into the parking lot.

Hiking directions: From the parking lot, walk towards the map and history exhibit at the trailhead. Follow the trail to the right around the fort walls. This path leads to the interior of the fort and past remnants of the guardrooms, barracks, cannon emplacements, the armory, and to red rock stairs that lead to lookout points along the coast. The trail loops back to the parking lot.

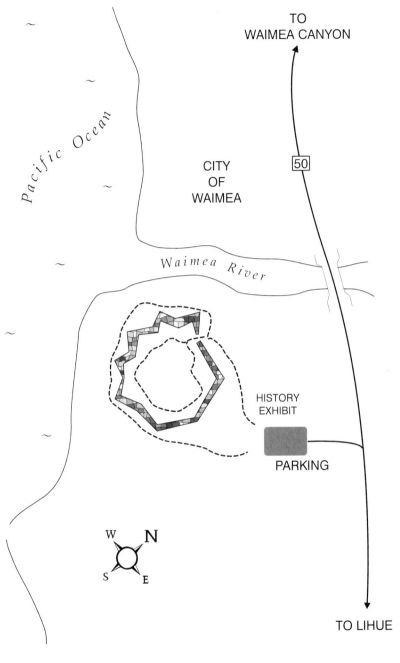

RUSSIAN FORT ELIZABETH

Hike 8
Kukuiolono Park and Japanese Garden

Hiking Distance: 1 mile round trip (plus garden stroll)
Hiking Time: 1 hour
Elevation Gain: Level hiking

Summary of hike: Kukuiolono Park has a one-mile nature loop, a Japanese garden with a stone footbridge and bonsai trees, a Hawaiian garden, and a lava rock garden (photo on page 23). The trail is surrounded with ironwood and eucalyptus trees and an abundance of flowers. Neighboring hillsides are dotted with beautiful homes and views of the Pacific Ocean.

Driving directions: From Lihue, drive 12 miles west on Highway 50 to Papalina Road in the town of Kalaheo. Turn left and continue one mile to Kukuiolono Park on the right. Turn right and park for the one-mile nature loop.
    For the Japanese Garden, drive up the park road a short distance to the parking lot.

Hiking directions: To hike along the one-mile nature loop, take the trail on the right closest to Papalina Road. This well-defined trail loops counterclockwise back to the parking area.
    For the Japanese, Hawaiian, and rock gardens, walk slightly uphill to the various walkways which loop through the gardens. All three gardens are bordered by a golf course.

Hike 9
Poipu Beach and Tidepools

Hiking Distance: 2 miles round trip
Hiking Time: 1 hour
Elevation Gain: Level hiking

Summary of hike: Poipu is the southernmost beach area in Kauai and is great for exploring. There are lava formations that house tidepools containing a variety of small fish, crabs, and hermit crabs (photo on page 22). There are also blowholes, ocean waves crashing against the cliffs, swimming bays, grassy park knolls, and sandy beaches. This is more than a hike—it is an excellent place to spend the day, enjoy water sports, or sunbathe.

Driving directions: From Lihue, drive 7 miles west on Highway 50. Turn left on Highway 520. Drive 3.3 miles to the end of the road. Turn right on Koloa Road, then a quick left on Poipu Road 0.1 mile ahead. Drive 2.5 miles on Poipu Road to Hoowili Road and turn right. Continue 0.2 miles to the ocean-front. Several parking lots are available.

Hiking directions: From the parking area, walk toward the ocean. Abundant tidepools and blowholes are located further down the beach to the east. (Head left from the parking lot.) Petroglyphs can be seen along the cliff walls at low tide, although recent property development has made access difficult. Walk along the lava formations and explore at your own pace.

Hike 10
Wailua Falls

Summary of hike: This is not a hike, but rather an opportunity to see a dramatic, powerful waterfall from the side of the road. This twin falls (cover photo) plunges eighty feet into a pool below surrounded by lush vegetation. It was filmed for the opening sequence of the *Fantasy Island* television series.

Driving directions: From Lihue, drive north on Highway 56 one mile to Highway 583. Turn left. A large highway sign will direct you. Continue four miles to the end of the road.

Hiking directions: On the right side of the road, Wailua Falls can be heard and seen. Hiking down to the base of the falls is dangerous and not recommended. Enjoy from a safe distance, and don't forget your camera!

Hike 11
Smith's Tropical Paradise
and Botanical Gardens
Open 8:30 a.m. - 4:30 p.m. everyday
There is an admission fee.

Hiking Distance: 1.5 miles
Hiking Time: 1 to 2 hours
Elevation Gain: Level hiking

Summary of hike: Look beyond the "tourist trap" aspects of this park and enjoy the superb botanical gardens and grounds. Located along the Wailua River, this 30-acre park has an abundance of plants, lagoons, and birds. The plants are identified with markers. Flowers and fruits from the trees are always in bloom. The sounds of birds echo throughout the park. You will share your hike with a variety of ducks, peacocks, and geese that also stroll the grounds. There is a Japanese garden on an island accessible via a footbridge (photo on page 22).

Driving directions: From Lihue, drive north 5.8 miles on Highway 56 to Wailua Road, located just before crossing the Wailua River and Highway 580. Turn left and continue on the Wailua Road 0.4 miles and park.

Hiking directions: After entering the botanical gardens, all the pathways intersect and are easy to follow. There are brochures with maps available to guide you.

Hike 12
Nounou Mountain (Sleeping Giant)
Kuamoo-Nounou Trail
to Valley Vista Hale

Hiking Distance: 1.5 miles round trip
Hiking Time: 1 hour
Elevation Gain: 150 feet

Summary of hike: This beautiful trail offers views from above the valley floor and of the surrounding mountains. Included in this hike is a wooden footbridge that crosses over Opaekaa Stream.

Driving directions: From Lihue, drive six miles north on Highway 56 to Kuamoo Road/Highway 580, the first intersection after crossing the Wailua River. Turn left and continue 2.4 miles to the parking area. The parking area is 0.7 miles past Opaekaa Falls on the right side of the road, directly across from Nelia Street.

Hiking directions: From the parking area, a sign on the fence marks the trailhead. Follow the tree-lined lane 0.2 miles to the footbridge crossing over Opaekaa Stream. After crossing, the trail curves left along a fence line, then winds its way up the side of Nounou Mountain into a dense forest. A short distance ahead, the trail breaks out of the forest to views of the Lihue Basin. At 0.75 miles you will be treated to Valley Vista Hale, a picnic shelter and overlook. This is your resting and turnaround point. If you would like to hike longer, the trail continues to the top of Nounou Mountain and eventually joins the West Side and East Side Trails. From Valley Vista Hale, return to your car along the same route.

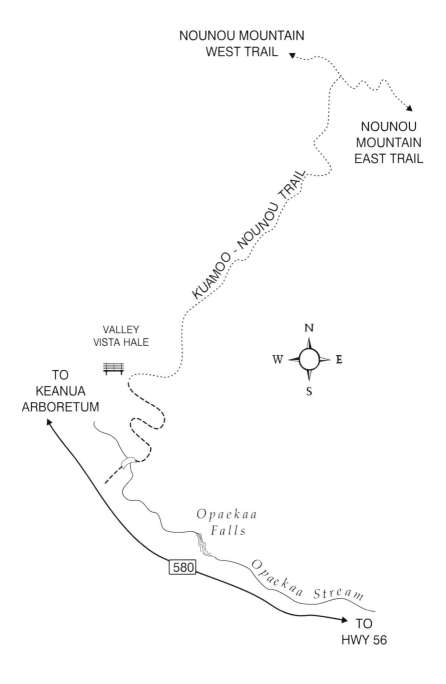

KUAMOO-NOUNOU TRAIL

Hike 13
Kuilau Ridge Trail to Overlook

Hiking Distance: 2.4 miles round trip
Hiking Time: 1.5 hours
Elevation Gain: 800 feet

Summary of hike: From the Keahua Arboretum, this trail climbs 1.2 miles up Kuilau Ridge to a picnic shelter that overlooks the surrounding mountains. The views are impressive.

Driving directions: From Lihue, drive six miles north on Highway 56 to Kuamoo Road/Highway 580, the first intersection after crossing the Wailua River. Turn left and continue 6.9 miles to the Keahua Arboretum. There are parking lots on either side of the road.

Hiking directions: From the Keahua Arboretum parking area, walk back along the road about 200 yards. The trailhead is on the left (north) side of the road. The six-foot wide trail (an old jeep trail) has metal 1/4 mile markers. The trail goes uphill all the way to the picnic shelter. The shelter and overlook is the resting and turnaround spot for this hike, although the trail continues further up the ridge and crosses the Moalepe Trail. To return to your car, hike back along the same trail.

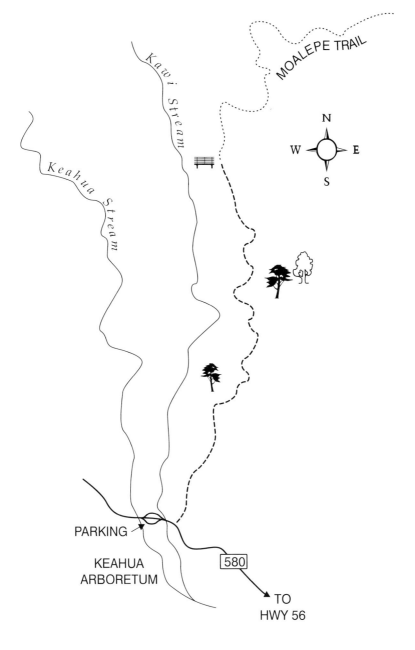

KUILAU RIDGE TRAIL

Hike 14
Keahua Arboretum
and Opaekaa Falls

Hiking Distance: 0.5 miles round trip
Hiking Time: 10 to 30 minutes
Elevation Gain: Level hiking

Summary of hike: Keahua Arboretum is divided into two areas by Keahua Stream, which runs through the middle. There is a short hike on each side. Both hikes follow the stream past two large swimming holes, picnic shelters, and expansive open lawns.

Driving directions: From Lihue, drive six miles north on Highway 56 to Kuamoo Road/Highway 580, the first intersection after crossing the Wailua River. Turn left and continue 6.9 miles to the Keahua Arboretum. There are parking lots on either side of the road.

En route, stop at Opaekaa Falls, just under two miles along Kuamoo Road. After a short walk you will be treated to a beautiful waterfall (photo on page 18).

Hiking directions: This is more of a stroll than a hike. From the parking area, the arboretum is on the right. You will wander along Keahua Stream through groves of gum trees, a variety of exotic plants, and hau thickets, all the while surrounded by mountains. The swimming holes are a short distance along Keahua Stream.

Hike 15
North Kapaa Ocean Walk

Hiking Distance: 2 miles round trip
Hiking Time: 1 hour
Elevation Gain: Level hiking

Summary of hike: This hike takes you along an old abandoned road that perches above the ocean. The views along this rugged coastline are magnificent. There is also a side trail up a grassy knoll to a point which overlooks the ocean in two directions.

Driving directions: From Lihue, drive north on Highway 56 between nine and ten miles to the north end of Kapaa. Park in the pullout on the right (ocean) side of the road by highway mile marker "9." The pullout is across the road from Kapaa Jodo Mission at Hauaala Road.

Hiking directions: From the parking pullout, walk south 50 feet to the old road that follows along the ocean ridge. Along the road, various paths lead down to the beach. Near the far end of the road, approximately 0.8 miles into the hike, is a large knoll with trails that lead down to the water and to the top of the ridge for views up and down the coastline. At one mile, the trail meets up again with Highway 56 by the Kapaa Stream bridge. Return to your car along the same path.

Hike 16
Kilauea Point National Wildlife Refuge
Open Mon. - Fri. 10 a.m. to 4 p.m.

Hiking Distance: 1/4 mile round trip
Hiking Time: 1 hour
Elevation Gain: Level hiking

Summary of hike: Kilauea Point National Wildlife Refuge and Kilauea Lighthouse are maintained by the U.S. Fish and Wildlife Service. Located at the northernmost point in Kauai, as well as Hawaii, this short hike is more of an "experience" than a hike. It offers the hiker breathtaking views of chiseled coastal cliffs, the crashing surf, a picturesque lighthouse, and hundreds of migratory birds on Mokuaeae Island, just off Kilauea Point (photo on page 23).

Driving directions: From Lihue, drive 24 miles north on Highway 56. Turn right on Kolo Road in the town of Kilauea. A sign to the lighthouse is posted at the turn. Drive 0.1 mile and turn left on Kilauea Road. Continue 1.6 miles to the end of the road. Turn left to the wildlife refuge entrance. The parking lot is a short distance ahead.

Hiking directions: From the parking area, walk towards the lighthouse to the north point and around the fenced perimeter. It is easy to find your way around without getting lost as the lighthouse is always within view.

Hike 17
Hanalei River Trail
Recommended: mosquito repellent

Hiking Distance: 3 miles round trip
Hiking Time: 1.5 hours
Elevation Gain: 200 feet

Summary of hike: This hike is a deep jungle experience. It will take you through tall bamboo forests, across streams, and into deep, dense foliage before ending at Kauai's largest river, the Hanalei River. White shoes are not recommended.

Driving directions: From Lihue, drive 30.5 miles north and west on Highway 56 towards Hanalei. After crossing a one-lane bridge, turn left. The sign at this turn reads "Hanalei National Wildlife Refuge." There are large cultivated taro fields on the right side of the road after the turn (photo on page 18). Continue for two miles on this road, and park near the hunter's check-in booth.

Hiking directions: From the parking area, hike along the road for about 20 minutes. The road changes from a muddy jeep trail to a foot trail. Watch on the left for a clearly visible trail that leads down through a dense forest to the first stream crossing. Rocks can be used as stepping stones to ford the stream. Continue through the bamboo forest to the second stream crossing. A short distance ahead are the banks of the Hanalei River. Return to your car along the same path.

Hike 18
Kee Beach to:
Na Pali Coast Overview
Hanakapiai Beach
Hanakapiai Falls

Hiking Distance	Time	Elevation Gain
To Na Pali Coast Overview:		
1.5 miles round trip	45 min.	500 feet
To Hanakapiai Beach:		
4 miles round trip	2.5 hrs.	1,000 feet
To Hanakapiai Falls:		
8 miles round trip	5 hrs.	1,750 feet

Summary of hike: The Na Pali Coast is an undeveloped, ancient route accessible only on foot. This magnificent, rugged coastline hike overlooks an endless series of primeval, emerald green valleys and steep cliffs that drop more than 3,000 feet to the turbulent sea. This hike covers the first portion of the 11-mile Kalalau Trail, which follows the Na Pali Coast along the cliff edge. The first valley along the trail is at Hanakapiai Beach. The side trail heading up this steep-walled valley to the 300-foot Hanakapiai Falls includes swimming pools and stream crossings—it should not be missed.

Driving directions: From Lihue, drive 42 miles north and west on Highway 56 to the end of the road. The drive is beautiful. The road hugs the coast past ocean bays, caves, streams, waterfalls, crosses over numerous one-lane bridges, and passes through the town of Hanalei. At the end of the road there are several places to park.

Hiking directions: From the parking area, the trailhead is on the inland side of the road by a large map and history exhibit that details the 11-mile trail to Kalalau Beach. The first mile climbs along an uneven lava rock trail to magnificent vistas of the isolated Na Pali Coast and its lush vegetation. The islands of Lehua and Ni'i hau are also visible from these lookouts as well as the crescent-shaped Kee Beach. The trail is usually wet and can be slippery. The second mile levels out until the descent to Hanakapiai Beach.

If you wish to continue another four miles round trip to Hanakapiai Falls, head inland into Hanakapiai Valley along the west side of the stream. The first mile is easy hiking; the second mile is more difficult due to erosion, mud, and stream crossings. There are swimming holes along the way. Near the falls, mist sprays onto the moss-covered rocks and thick vegetation. The valley narrows and the trail leads directly to the falls.

A map of these hikes is included on the next page.

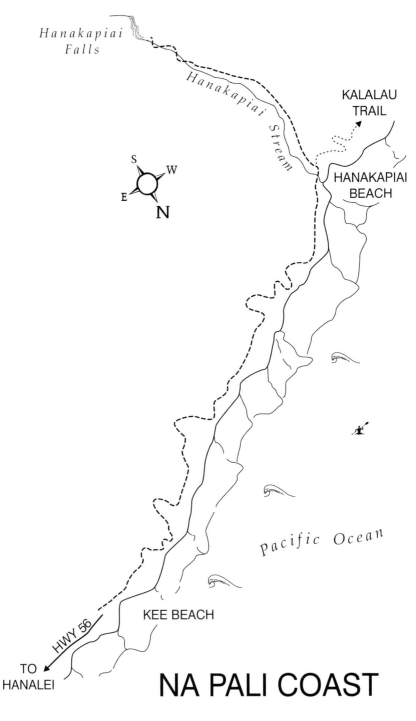

Hanakapiai Falls

Hanakapiai Stream

KALALAU TRAIL

HANAKAPIAI BEACH

S W
E N

Pacific Ocean

KEE BEACH

HWY 56

TO HANALEI

NA PALI COAST

NOTES

Bibliography

Bisignani, J.D. *Hawaii Handbook.*
   Chico, CA: Moon Publication, 1989.

Chisholm, Craig. *Kauai Hiking Trails.*
   Lake Oswego, OR: Fernglen Press, 1991.

Hadley, Thelma. *Road Guide to Kokee and Waimea Canyon
   State Parks.*
   Honolulu: The Bess Press, 1988.

Morey, Kathy. *Kauai Trails.*
   Berkeley, CA: Wilderness Press, 1991.

Riegert, Ray. *Hidden Hawaii.* 7th ed.
   Berkeley, CA: Ulysses Press, 1993.

Smith, Robert. *Hiking Kauai.* 4th ed.
   Long Beach, CA: Hawaiian Outdoor Adventures Publication,
   1989.

Smith, Rodney N. *Hawaii: A Walker's Guide.*
   Edison, NJ: Hunter Publication, no year listed.

Valier, Kathy. *On the Na Pali Coast.*
   Honolulu: University of Hawaii Press, 1988.

Information Sources

Division of State Parks
P.O. Box 1671
3060 Eiwa St. Room 306
Lihue, Kauai, HI 96766

Division of Forestry and Wildlife
P.O. Box 1671
3060 Eiwa St.
Lihue, Kauai, HI 96766
(808) 245-4433

Dept. of Parks and Recreation
4280A Rice St. Bldg. B
Lihue, Kauai, HI 96766
(808) 245-1881

Kokee Natural History Museum
P.O. Box 100
Kekaha, Kauai, HI 96752
(808) 335-9975

Kokee Lodge
P.O. Box 819
Waimea, Kauai, HI 96796
(808) 335-6061

Smith's Tropical Paradise
(808) 822-4654 822-9599

The Nature Conservancy of Hawaii
1116 Smith St. Room 201
Honolulu, HI 96817
(808) 537-4508

Hawaiian Visitor Bureaus:

On Kauai:
  3016 Umi St.
  Lihue, HI 96799
  (808) 245-3971
On Oahu:
  2270 Kalakaua Ave.
  Room 801
  Honolulu, HI 96815
  (808) 923-1811
In Los Angeles:
  3440 Wilshire Blvd.
  Room 502
  Los Angeles, CA 90010
  (213) 385-5301
In San Francisco:
  50 California St.
  Suite 450
  San Francisco, CA 94111
In Chicago:
  180 North Michigan Ave.
  Suite 1031
  Chicago, IL 60601
In New York:
  441 Lexington Ave.
  Suite 1003
  New York, NY 10017
  (212) 986-9203
In Washington, D.C.:
  1511 K Street N.W.
  Suite 519
  Washington D.C. 20005

Other Day Hike Guidebooks

___ Day Hikes on Oahu $6.95
___ Day Hikes on Maui 8.95
___ Day Hikes on Kauai. 8.95
___ Day Trips on St. Martin. 9.95
___ Day Hikes in Denver 6.95
___ Day Hikes in Boulder, Colorado 8.95
___ Day Hikes in Steamboat Springs, Colorado. 8.95
___ Day Hikes in Summit County, Colorado 8.95
___ Day Hikes in Aspen, Colorado 7.95
___ Day Hikes in Yosemite National Park
     25 Favorite Hikes 8.95
___ Day Hikes in Yellowstone National Park
     25 Favorite Hikes 7.95
___ Day Hikes in the Grand Tetons and Jackson Hole, WY.... 7.95
___ Day Hikes in Los Angeles
     Malibu to Hollywood 8.95
___ Day Hikes in the Beartooth Mountains
     Red Lodge, Montana to Yellowstone National Park 8.95

These books may be purchased at your local bookstore or they will be glad to order them. For a full list of titles available directly from ICS Books, call toll-free 1-800-541-7323. Visa or Mastercard accepted.

- -

Please include $2.00 per order to cover postage and handling. Please send the books marked above. I enclose $ _____

Name _____

Address _____

City _____ State _____ Zip _____

Credit Card # _____ Exp. _____

Signature _____

1-800-541-7323

Distributed by:
ICS Books, Inc.
1370 E. 86th Place, Merrillville, In. 46410
1-800-541-7323 • Fax 1-800-336-8334

About the Author

An avid hiker for many years, Robert Stone has found the Hawaiian Islands a hiking paradise. He has hiked and photographed extensively throughout Asia, Europe, the Caribbean, Hawaiian Islands, and the United States. When not traveling, Robert makes his home in the Rocky Mountains of Montana.